Praise for

River Inside the River

"For four decades, Gregory Orr has been among a small handful of poets who make me proud to be among their generation of writers. Orr's new book is a wonder, exploring such weighty themes as the sources of love, the sources of mourning, the working of redemption and memory, the ways in which these give rise to poetic utterance . . . all in language as light as airborne thistledown. For such powerful lyric importance to come from such small deft breaths requires both mastery and magic; both are plentiful here, on every page."

—Albert Goldbarth

"This is a book that is both reflective and ecstatic. It embraces an extended meditation but casts a spell through lyric impulse. It is incendiary, inventive, incantatory. It is erotic. It is, indeed, irresistible."   —Ilya Kaminsky

"Gregory Orr's poems have always had the stunning ability to place mindfulness almost instantly back inside the mind. Once again, a river inhabits its true banks, and a soul, its boundless person."   —Naomi Shihab Nye

"Orr's spiritual journey continues with healing words that embrace the myth of creation and the redemptive power of language. . . . American poet Gregory Orr's 10th collection,

River Inside the River, sees him continue his mission to write a poetry of authentic spiritual affirmation through the narrative of myth. For Orr, the reading and writing of poetry is essential to spiritual existence." —Rowan Righelato, *Guardian* (UK)

"With his new book, *River Inside the River: Poems,* Gregory Orr set a high bar for himself. His intention: to write three lengthy pieces that combine the intensity of lyric poetry with the thematic scope of narrative and myth. Fortunately, Orr's literary talent and personal experience make him the ideal poet to realize such an ambitious project."

—Michelle Aldredge, Gwarlingo

"Orr ranks as a great seer, casting a mythic spell over the reader with his technically attuned verse."

—Arlice Davenport, *Wichita Eagle*

River
Inside the
River

River
Inside the
River

THREE LYRIC SEQUENCES

Gregory Orr

W. W. NORTON & COMPANY　　NEW YORK • LONDON

For information about permission to reproduce selections from this book,
write to Permissions, W. W. Norton & Company, Inc.,
500 Fifth Avenue, New York, NY 10110

For information about special discounts for bulk purchases, please contact
W. W. Norton Special Sales at specialsales@wwnorton.com or 800-233-4830

Manufacturing by Courier Westford
Production manager: Louise Mattarelliano

Library of Congress Cataloging-in-Publication Data

Orr, Gregory.
[Poems. Selections]
River inside the river : three lyric sequences / Gregory Orr. — First edition.
pages cm
ISBN 978-0-393-23974-4 (hardcover)
I. Title.
PS3565.R7R58 2013
811'.54—dc23

2012050743

ISBN 978-0-393-34995-5 pbk.

W. W. Norton & Company, Inc.
500 Fifth Avenue, New York, N.Y. 10110
www.wwnorton.com

W. W. Norton & Company Ltd.
Castle House, 75/76 Wells Street, London W1T 3QT

1 2 3 4 5 6 7 8 9 0

Contents

Eden and After

The City of Poetry

River Inside the River

Eden
and
After

To Speak

It hadn't occurred
To God
To use words.
He'd simply thought
The world
Into being.
Merely imagined
Those animals,
That shrub.

But He *was*
Proud
Of what He'd done.

He didn't want
To boast,
But still He felt
An urge.

He cleared His throat
And spoke.

To See

True, as time passed,
Adam's eyes
Would weary the world
With looking, would
Wear away
The sheen it wore
As sheath and shield.

But now, in his first gaze,
Each object gleamed—
Slick and shiny
With its afterbirth of light.

It shone in watery silence
With only sight
Connecting
It to him,
And him to everything.

To Write

What was inside Adam
Swirled about, but outside
All was still and held
Its shape.
        How negotiate
Between these worlds:
The one that whirled,
The one that waited
To be designated?

Lifting a stick, he drew
Marks in the dirt—
Idle doodles and arbitrary
Scratches.
        Animals
approached,
Leaned over his shoulder.

They wondered at what he wrote.

To Name

God wanted labels
That would stick
To fur or bark or leaf.

Hadn't he given Adam
A tongue?
Why not have him name?

The Parade

As they paraded past
Adam named them all,
That is—all he saw.

Some were too busy
To heed God's call;
Others were hidden.

Some, like the worm,
Were both:
                    its mouth
Was full, it was chewing
Its way through earth—

A pink needle tugging
A black thread of tunnel,
Stitching a dark shroud.

To Noun

Nouns were a giant
Confining—
Adam felt the sounds
He made
Build bars around
The things he saw.

It hurt and thrilled him
To see how meekly
Each thing
Entered that cage.

How snug it fit;
How smug he felt.

To Verb

The beasts were beasting,
The birds, birding about—

Everywhere Adam looked
He saw moving tokens
Of becoming's task—
Clearly their glory
Was spoken as motion,
But to praise them
He needed
More precise words.

Floating, sniffing,
Gliding, drifting—

Burrowing, soaring,
Grunting, roaring . . .

He'd poked among the shrubs
And noted they were stable.
Now, he gazed at birds flying
Wherever they whimmed.

Maybe his tongue was a root,
But weren't his verbs wings?

Eve

That rib—a bone
Curved
Like a fish-hook—
When it
Was removed
It pulled out
Part of his heart . . .

Often, the best dreams
Vanish most quickly—
Glitter and gone.

But here she stood:
Palpable, complete.

And if her open hand
Moved, hesitant,
Toward his
It was no mirror trick—
It was felicity.

That they were different
Adam could see.

His mind created
Difference
As it dreamed and now,
Awake, it sought
To close
The distance it had made.

He watched her walk
Away, walk down
The path that curved
And disappeared.

Cry that rose so sudden
In his throat to burst
That eerie silence—
That cry became her name.

To Do

God made a big to-do
About their doing,
And it's true—
Those early days
Were festive,
Given each deed
They did was done
For the first time,
Was essence.
                    To boast,
To sleep, to flirt:
Each verb had dew
Upon it, and was new.

To Feel

There was a meadow
At the garden's center
Where a tree grew.
She liked to sit there
With her back against
The trunk.
           Nothing
Unusual about
That tree: gray,
Undistinguished bark,
Tiny leaves like lids
Held tightly shut . . .

Adam watched her
From the meadow's edge.

"Forlorn" entered
His mind. But was it
The meadow or the tree
That grew there?

Was it him or her
Who felt that feeling
So distinct
It had the taste of bitter fruit?

To Long

How beautiful they were,
Adam thought—
These beasts and birds;
These tall grasses
And flowering trees.

And yet, how full
The universe—
As if there were no room
For words he ached to say.

Shouted aloud, they
Might displace
The very things
He wished to celebrate.

Therefore, he sang
A dense and wordless song
That filled the only
Emptiness he knew:

Inside him,
Near his heart
Where a rib had been removed.

To No/To Know

God's language
Lessons usually
Began with "No."

As if prohibition
Gave Him pleasure.

Eve liked to say "Yes,"
Which was all
Adam needed to know.

To Say

Saying itself was a kind
Of seizing with love.

Eve taught him that—
She for whom prayer
Was praising
What was there—

The world
Spread out before her,
What else should she adore?

To Choose

God planned a static planet,
With plants that bore
No offspring—as if
Acts had no consequence.

But Eve was there to change
All that by choosing . . .
To show Adam losing
Was illusion
If you took it all inside you:
The bright fruit, the garden's
Beauty, the day's delight
And the night sky with its stars . . .

Show him how, within you,
It would ripen
And give birth to things
Beyond yourself and your imaginings.

To Smell

Adam bent over the first rose.
He only meant
To breathe it briefly,
But its odor
Opened secret doors
Inside him and he
Closed his eyes
And pressed his nose
Deeper into its redolent folds.

To Fuck

Not a subject God
Knew much about—
His bodiless body
Immune to its charms.

They were on their own
In this department
And chose to trust
How part responded
To part—not just
Cock to cunt
And cunt to cock,
But also heart to heart.

To Come

He went; she came.
It was her turn;
Then, his.
They both arrived
At the same place—
A quiet space
No bigger
Than a smile
They found
Inside them when
The throbbing stopped.

To Embrace

With their embrace
They chose
Each other,
Which is
To choose death
And all that comes
Before it:
Sufferings
And joys
And infinite
Unintended harms.

Large choice
For such small arms.

To Go

Who wouldn't be alarmed
To see the tulip's
Fleshy petals
Wilt and fall?

Eve felt her heart
Contract.

"So be it," she prayed
Who knew full well
The gravity
Of what it was
That she beheld:

How it was definitive,
Beyond recall.

To Stray

Words were what set them off—

Set them off
From the other
Beasts,
      Set them on
Their own path.
          Path
That wound
Its way beneath
The trees of Eden
Like a slow stream,
Like a wound
Worn in the earth
By feet repeating—

Always to the garden's edge.

To Leave

Mostly, the birds in Eden
Sat on branches,
Sunned their wings all day
And sang from dawn
Till dark.
          To fly
Seldom occurred to them,
But when they heard
God's shout,
Huge flocks lifted
From the trees as one—
As if half the leaves
In Paradise had come undone.

To Squint

Adam and Eve
Stumbled
Into the open,
Into a sun
Brighter than
They'd ever known
In Eden.
       Wince
At dazzle,
Bow the head
And lift the hand
To shield—
A narrowing
Of sight
To help you
Stay alive:
That spot of earth
Where foot
Will fall
And a few inches
On either side.

Departure

To the trees, leaving
Came naturally—
A green extension
Of their being.

But for Adam and Eve
There was no
Precedent.

It meant
A tearing loose.

True, the mind
Might circle back
As memory—
What leash
Could hold it?
What wall
Could keep it out?

But to hear the gates
Clang shut behind you
Was to know the sound of final.

To Weep

Tears were forbidden in Eden—
God didn't want the soil embittered.

Beyond the gates, they were free
To weep.
     And weeping became
A form of freedom:
It meant you felt; it meant you had a self.

To Notice

In Eden, Adam
Had been so busy
Making up smug
Nouns of dominion,
He hadn't watched
What each beast
And bird was up to.

Now he had time
To study them
And saw they wanted
The few, same things:
Peace and quiet for most;
For others, a piece
Of food to pursue
Then a shady place
To rest
And chew it over.

Adam chewed it over,
Thought it through—
It dawned on him
That outside Eden
They were eaters or eaten.

To Journey

They were alive;
They had survived
God's wrath
With bodies intact.

Now they had new
Worlds to explore,
New words to learn . . .

True, they'd start
With "suffering"
And "dust"
But after that
And over the next hill,
Who knew what?

Still

Still, he heard
The gates slam;
Still, he saw
The angel brandish
Its flaming sword—
Scene seared
In memory—
To have seen it,
And to see it still.

The way her heart
Beat every time
They climbed a hill.

The way her lungs
Hurt as they neared
Each crest.

How could she still
Her fears?

To Hope

Beyond the next dune
Or the next . . .

Beyond that distant
Mountain
Where the clouds
Crowded . . .

First, he spoke
With certainty:
What they would find.

Later, only silently
To himself,
And that was hope.

When

When the wind blew,
You couldn't stand still—
Under you, sand shifted;
Around you, dunes rose
And fell in waves
Like the still-undiscovered sea.

You had to change your footing.
You had to move, too.

Close

Each evening, they
Lay down:
The one
Beside the other.

In the night,
He heard her breath,
Felt her heart
Beneath her breast.

To feel her body
Close to his
Sometimes induced
A dizziness,
Sometimes a deep ease.

To Love

Grieving came from leaving Eden
But leaving Eden was not grief—
It was a lesson in lessening—
How things, diminishing,
Become more precious.

Water seeps from two hands
Cupped to hold it—
Skin tight against skin
As lips seek it:
That liquid
That is life
And slips
Away.

To Understand

Out there, it was an earthly
Garden that they made
And therefore never
Changeless.
                        Whatever
Flowered had to fade,
That's why sorrow
And pleasure grew
On the same tree—
The one Eve loved the most,

The one she sat beneath
In the softer seasons,
Listening as the small birds called
And the nearby deer
Tore the grass with their teeth.

To Say/To Save

Eve sensed this
Was something
Words could do
In a fallen world:

Move a thing's
Death
Briefly outside it.

Now, her praising
Had new purpose:

As she spoke aloud
Each flower's name
She felt her saying save.

Sometimes

Sometimes the way
A setting sun
Gilds high-piled
Clouds reminds them,
As if Eden was
An island in the sky.

And yet, they seldom
Miss it, who have
Each other now
And all the world besides.

Now

Eden's empty now.
The animals
That lived there—
All have left.

They missed
The words that
Held them there
As in a web.

They also missed
Those human voices
Calling,
Those bright threads . . .

To Build

No longer could they rest
Each night inside
God's breath
As in a tent that kept
Them from the cold.

All this was new,
Was after-Eden.
No longer could
They sleep beneath
The trees, trusting
Branches not to break.

It was a habitation
They had to make:
Four walls and a roof—
A place to live,
A world inside the world.

The City
of Poetry

It would have erased everything human—
The deep snow of oblivion—
If those before us hadn't kept
Poking up the huts of poems.

And then: small houses
Huddled in a settlement.

And soon it became a village,
And next it was a town.

And now it makes its own weather.

Now, the winds walk around it.
Now the clouds bow.
                    Now the snow
Recedes from the shining city.

Some say Adam and Eve
Made it—
She from her praise,
He from his grief.

Some say they built it
Out of their
Fallenness—
He with his praise,
She from her grief.

Raising the walls,
Laying the roof;
She with her praise,
He with his grief—
Building the first house of song.

She with her grief,
He with his praise—
Making the holy human city,
Making the wholly human city.

Bored in grade school,
I lingered inside
While my classmates
Raced to the playground
At recess.
        Alone
In the room, I yielded
To the pull of the globe.

Above its whirling surface
My finger hovered.

The unknown, the unknown—
Where it stopped
I would someday go.

I killed my younger brother
In a hunting accident
when I was twelve.

Two years later, my mother
Took sick and died
In a single night.

My world closed in
On all sides.
I could hardly breathe.

If someone had told me
then . . .

A place where every poem
Is a house;
And every house, a poem.

When I first came here
Fifty years ago—
The moment I arrived,
I knew this city was my home.

Eighteen and a volunteer
In the Movement,
I was kidnapped at gunpoint
In rural Alabama
And imprisoned
In a solitary cell
In a murderous town.
                    Oddly,
After the beatings and threats,
They let me keep a book of Keats.

I was sick and scared. It seemed
Likely I would die there.

I read his nightingale ode—
How he rose above his woes.

The poem was my ladder:
Rungs and lifts of escape.

I read it at dusk, climbing
With each line.
And I was there with that bird
I could just glimpse
By shinnying up
The bars of my cell:

Mockingbird in the magnolia
Across the moonlit road.

(Hayneville, Alabama, 1965)

Who needs plaques
Or nameplates when
The houses themselves
Are so distinctive?

Blake's cottage easy
To recognize
By the angels dancing
All day on the roof.

From the drainspouts
Of Baudelaire's villa
Gargoyles leer.

There's an orchid boat
Moored in the canal
Out back of Li Po's.

And Whitman's house
Is crowned with sod,
With grass deep-rooted
And swaying in the wind.

Dickinson's has two large
Windows on the second floor:
Staring, startled, intelligent eyes.

A thousand roads lead to it,
And ten thousand paths.
Its gates are always open
Night and day.
      Oldest
And newest city on earth—
Young poets creating
Almost impossible structures:
Tall, postmodern, made
Entirely of polycarbon
Or mylar.
      While scholars
Digging into sandstone cliffs
Find pillars carved
With love poems in hieroglyphics.

Until I heard Neruda read
His poems aloud,
I never even knew
I could fly
To the city of poems.

He had arrived
That day on a plane
For his first visit
To Manhattan, the city
Of Whitman, one of his heroes.

"Vienes volando," he intoned—
"You come flying"—
Refrain from an elegy
In which he summoned
A friend's spirit over the Andes.

I stood in the crowded room
And remembered my own loved dead.

That was forty years ago, and yet
I can still hear his sonorous voice—
"Vienes volando"—
And whenever I hear it
I'm transported again to that other city.

(YM-YWHA Poetry Center, New York City, 1966)

Tang of salt in the walls
And boards—
Not from harbor
Or shore,
But the boundless sea
Of grief,
That ocean inside us.

Still, the maker
Didn't weep
As she framed
Her house.
He never paused
To sob
As he laid out
The flooring.

Born of sorrow,
Yet the joy in making it.

You're invited to visit
A particular poem—
To go often enough
To become familiar
With each of its rooms;
To nose around in the attic
And explore its cellar.

Encouraged to arrive early
And greet dawn
Through various windows;
To linger long enough
To watch the shadows
Arrive toward evening.

Only a guest, yet
Welcome to stay forever.
To stay as long as you want;
As long as it gives you pleasure.

From the outside, these row houses
Look pretty much the same,
As if the whole street were sonnets.
But you know that inside some

People are fucking; in others,
Sitting down to supper or drinking
Themselves into a stupor
While staring at a photo on the wall.

Narrow confines of the formal poem—
Yet within you, every emotion
Expressed, every known drama
Enacted. And all of it happens

With such intensity—it's a wonder
Your walls don't burst asunder.

So many brought here by water,
Though seldom a cruise ship or yacht.
Most in the small boat of self.

Some after long struggle—
Strenuously rowing upstream.
Others, tossed on the rocks,
Or washed up, half-dead, on the shore.

There's only one river
That flows
Through the city,
But different poems
Call it different names.

In some it's Lethe,
River of oblivion;
In others, it's Time
Itself—that stream
That moves through
All poems and laps
At the banks
Of words, slowly eroding.

Some name it after
A childhood brook
As if its current
Had moved alongside
Their own from birth,
As if they both emerged
From the same source.

Others dub it something
Exotic, as if to say:
You are a river no one
Has seen,

Except in imagination—
You are the color
Of my longing,
Which is deep and pure.

Love overwhelms us.

Or death takes

One more
Of those
We cherish most.

Where else?

Where else can we go?

It's not all spun sugar and gossamer—
On the contrary, everything's there,
Including deepest grief and horror.

The city's like that—joy and squalor
Are its meat and drink.
It's not all spun sugar and gossamer.

I mean, it *would* be if that's what life were,
But this world is full of suffering and pain,
Including deepest grief and horror,

And so the city is also. Part of its allure
Is that its poems can speak the truth,
Which isn't all spun sugar and gossamer.

Ask any poet why this is. Talk to him or her
About why many poems blithely
Include deepest grief and horror—

If they're halfway honest, I'm sure
They'll tell you this city, like the human heart,
Contains it all—spun sugar and gossamer,
But also deepest grief and even horror.

Consider François Villon—
Murderer and thief
If half the rumors are true.
How did he come to live here
As if he were respectable?

My best guess is that he wrote
"Où sont les neiges d'antan"—
"Where are the snows
Of yesteryear"—a refrain
That followed a list
Of famous beauties he once knew.

I don't claim he was the first
To lament that bodily beauty
Vanishes like melting snow,
But when you think of the city,
Remember Villon.

Coleridge was only a little stoned
When he first glimpsed it . . .

Agonies of procrastination—
They're all forgotten
In the city.

He's finished it at last
And lives inside it:

That stately pleasure dome
He and Kubla Khan
Began so many years ago.

From a distance,
It glistens
As if marble
Was the only stone
Any poet ever used.

But closer, you see
It's coated
With grime
As if the whole
City was built
Downwind
From Blake's
"Dark Satanic mills."

A good rain
Will always cleanse it.

Or even
A single tear
Falling on a single page.

Not everyone in the city
Sleeps in a house—Rimbaud
Vagabonds about, a youth
With backpack, dog,
And homemade tattoos.
His poems too restless
To settle; appearing
As phrases on walls—
Bold and disturbing,
Making us uneasy—
A sacred/demonic grafitti.

And Sappho, whose known
To us only in fragments—
It follows that she doesn't
Have a house—only a gown
And that's in tatters.
Linen like gauze,
And where it's torn,
Revealing the body beneath—
Slender and passionate.
But don't pity her—
It's a garment that flatters.

Nor will Rumi permit a roof—
He won't have any barrier
Between the infinite and him.
You'll find him in a great

Open space, where he dances
On one foot, then the other.
You could say his house
Is the pillar of dust
His spinning raises up,
And he stands inside it, singing.

And Trakl, each night after dark,
Stumbles into the park
And clambers up into
The outstretched, marble arms
Of an angel
And curls up in a ball.
Wadded poems stuffed
In his clothes will keep him
Warm.
       Angel of cocaine,
Angel of his suicide sister,
Angel of atonement—
Who knows, who knows?
He sleeps like a child
After a fever.
He sleeps as if all were forgiven.

In the middle of my life,
In the middle of the city,
I got lost.

I'd exhausted
Certain districts—
Knew them by heart.
But I was afraid
To explore
And paused there
A long, dark moment.

All my guides
Were gone—
Those older poets
Who seemed to know
Where I should go.

I was terrified
To wander
Down unnamed alleys,
To risk discoveries
I couldn't predict.

I was only half-alive:
Shameful fact for a poet.

I was afraid to imagine,
Afraid to act.

Sometimes, the river
Seems wide
As the sky;

Other times, narrow
As a ditch
I step across
Without stretching.

Sometimes, I stand
All day
On its banks,
Yearning, yet
Never see the other shore.

Sometimes, it's thin
As the artery
Throbbing in my temple.

White flag
Of the city—

No ensign
Of surrender,
But radiant
Sign of desire:
Blank sheet
Of the page—
Bed with covers
Thrown back,

Ready
For the wars of love.

"O, thou opening O . . ."
Roethke
Begins his ode.

O, poem
Of the beloved.

O, beautiful body
Whose every
Orifice is holy.

O, porch
Made of breath,
House made of air.

The door
We go through—
So small.

The rooms
We enter—immense.

Some as ephemeral
As the coins
Minted in the city—
Vanishing
Like snowflakes
In your open palm.

Not all poems seek
Permanence.

Think of those
Lovers' couplets
That wove tall
Meadow grass
Into an afternoon's bower.

Some, forever;
Others, just one sweet hour.

Whenever its enemies besiege it,
The city transforms itself
Into heaps of scrolls
And huge twig-piles of words.

Once they've set them on fire
(A huge conflagration
That lights up the night sky),
They dance and exult,
Enjoying the blaze enormously.

And when the flames die down,
They prod the embers
And feel proud of their power.

And before long, they're bored
And climb back on their high
Horses or jeeps and return
To their forts and towers.

They've hardly been gone an hour,
When there it is again—that marvelous city.

Neglected for decades—
Dust on the floor,
Cobwebs in every corner.

Yet just as it was:
No word moved
So much as an inch.

Waiting to be rediscovered.

Sometimes, entering
The house of a poem,
You're greeted
By your other self—

That person you
Could have become
Had things gone
Differently.
                    Or even
Who you *really* are,
Though it's been kept
Secret, even from you.

Under the pretext
Of a guided tour,
He tries to convey
An urgent message.

It's crucial but elusive,
Not even in the words
But in what you intuit
From hints and gestures.

It's something on which
Both your lives depend.

That poem I call
"My Mother's House":
Everything I can
Remember
Crammed inside it:
Parrots and a bowl
Of peaches, the bright
Rug my aunt wove.

Shadows also.
Mysteries and secrets.
Corridors only ghosts patrol.

I sat on the bank of a pond
Behind a farmhouse I rented.
A summer breeze brought
The fragrance of pines.

Shoreside reeds parted
And my cat approached,
Daintily placing each paw.
She sat beside me, looked out
At the water and began to purr.

That occurred thirty years ago.

I find it now in the city. I must
Have turned that day into words.

(Earlysville, Virginia, 1978)

The life I live,
The one I hoped
To live—
How seldom
They coincide.

Sometimes, briefly,
They do;
Sometimes, in the city.

As I say aloud the opening line
Of my favorite poem,
My breath calms.
                              Soon,
The sounds I make
Set my hands dancing,
And next my feet
Begin to move.

Before I know it,
I'm walking again
In the city.
My stride's jaunty,
My legs feel strong.

I'm an old man
Made young again
By the poems I love.

Reciting them as I saunter along.

River
Inside the
River

… As an anthologist might gather
all the poems and songs
that matter
into a single book—the Book
that is the resurrection
of the body of the beloved,
which is the world.

The Book said we were mortal;
It didn't say we had to be morbid.

The Book said the beloved died,
But also that she comes again,
That he's reborn as words.

The Book said: everything perishes.
The Book said: that's why we sing.

Knowing life grinds us,
And dust
Is what we'll become.

Sensing, likewise,
That the moral
Of our story
Has to do
With being mortal.

Yet love grounds us.

And the beloved
Grows in us:
We are her slow cocoon.

And the poem is a door;
The song, a little window.

Like fireflies hovering
Around a summer oak,
Words crowd around
The beloved—
Respectful, yet eager.

They sense her infinite
Possibility; they're drawn
To his heart, large as a star.

Only some will be summoned,
Only some will be sung.

Each of us standing at a particular
Spot we favor—our own location
Along the mortal shore.

Scanning the horizon.
                              There it is!
We watch the boat of the Book
Float by.
                    All our beloveds on board.
Waving from the deck,
Calling out our name.
Some of them singing.
                              Some just
Gazing at us with that look we loved.

Yearning for permanence, and who wouldn't?
Longing to believe it will last forever,
But what does? Nothing I know of.

Even the things that seem to stand still
Flow slowly into other forms.

The beloved's first and only lesson:
Everything that is, becomes.

Bald, high-domed Taoist sage
Holding the Peach of Immortality
In one hand, a hiking staff in the other.

I like to think he's reciting a poem,
One that begins: "To eat a peach . . ."
One that stresses its succulence,
And how the sticky, delicious juice
Dribbles down your chin.

He's fresh from a rendezvous
With the beloved. Peach
And poem—both are her tokens.

Most poems
From mouth
And tongue,
This one
From teeth:
Playful nip
On your thigh.

Hours later,
It still hurts;
Next day,
A bruise,
Tender
To the touch.

Whenever
You rub it
You think of her.

"Why not a brief respite?"
I plead with the beloved.

"Bad idea," she insists:
"There's a world out there
You need to see, to be."

"But I'm tired," I whine.

"Sorry," the beloved
Responds, "you'll rest
When you're done.
Meanwhile, there's a word
In here (he's pointing
Toward his heart)
You need to become."

Note to self: remember
What Emerson said
Of Thoreau—
That he loved the low
In nature:
   Muskrats
And crickets, suckers
And frogs.
   Not stars.

Songs of the carnal,
Songs of what we are.

Not to lead us *away*
From the world
But deeper into it—
To persuade us
She *is* it.

Not all of it, not
Vastness,
But some one thing
We love—

Isn't that what he's become?

Cat curled asleep
On my lap—
Beloved
As love-sponge.

Dog gazing up
From the floor—
All calm
And liquid eyes—
All fountain.

That surplus,
That overflow—
Give it away,
Give it away.

How much more
Than we
Can absorb
The beloved bestows.

No tome so obscure
That it must become
The beloved's tomb.

Open the cover:
Bird that she is:
She's flying; he's flown.

Today a letter arrived,
Sent from the city
Of poems—
The beloved
Summoning us.

The contents lucid,
The return address
Blurred by tears.

We must hurry there.
We must search
The city, high and low.

Even if it takes years.

So many to choose from,
But some are just words.

Couldn't the beloved tell us
In which poem she's hiding?

Couldn't he hint at where
He's concealed himself?

Must I read everything?
Must I search years?

Why not? Why not?
Easily found; easily forgot.

I know now the beloved
Has no fixed abode,
That each body
She inhabits
Is only a temporary
Home.
   That she
Casts off forms
As eagerly
As lovers shed clothes.

I accept that he's
Just passing through
That flower
Or that stone.

And yet, it makes
Me dizzy—
The way he hides
In the flow of it,
The way she shifts
In fluid motions,
Becoming other things.

I want to stop him—
If only briefly.
I want to lure her

To the surface
And catch her
In this net of words.

Memorize those lines you love,
As you tried to memorize
Every part of the beloved's body.

Memorize, and then forget—
Let them vanish
Into that dark that's large as death.

They'll come again
When you most need, least expect.

When the coffin closed at last,
When flames consumed it,
Your eyes were useless—

What tears could put out
That fire?
                And so, you shut them.
So, you let the lids of your eyes
Close over the beloved's body.

For a while now—darkness.

And what you see will be inside you.

Set beside the world's
Vast sufferings,
Our loss was small.

We know that.
And yet, for us,
It altered everything.

Taught us "much"
Is no measure.
Taught us depth is all.

Hardening the heart
In order
To survive,

Becoming the stone
Whose blossom
Opens inward,

Or the mountaintop
Pine bowed
By a ceaseless wind—

All his joy kept inside,
As if holding her breath
An entire lifetime.

Sorrow is good;
Tears are good.
But too much
Grief erodes.

What if all
The soft soil
Washes away
And only hard
Furrows remain?

Then what?

Then what can grow in us?

First, there was shatter.
Then, aftermath.

Only later and only slowly
We gathered words
Against our loss.

But last was not least,
Last was not least of these.

That song on the jukebox—
An emissary
The beloved sent—
It's only doing
Its two-part job:

First, it breaks our heart;

Then it promises
Never to mend it again.

Intimacy not yet
A science:

No one knows
How or why
Bodies come close
Then recede.

One day, the abyss
Between you
Is infinite,
And distance
Mocks your shout.

The next, a whisper's loud.

The beloved came,
Then vanished.
Nothing beautiful stays.

Nothing beautiful
Stays the same;
Everything changes,
Everything
Dances away.

We've only
This moment
To bless him
And send him on his way.

Quick, with our lips
We form our kiss:
A poem is what they say.

Lucky poets us,
To whom
Sappho bequeathed
Her voodoo lute

That we might name
And praise
And raise from oblivion's
Grave

All that we most love.

Lead of the heart;
Gold of song.

Alchemy of grief
The poem performs.

He was hidden, then
Discovered.
She was lost,
And then recovered.

If these are games
The beloved plays,
What are the rules?

Risk all. Feel all.
Hold nothing back.

How do I win?

How can you lose?

Dancing to her song
From the day I was born.

More and more proper
As I grew older.

Now, I'm downright
Solemn as I plod along.

You'd never know
I was anything but sober,

Yet deep inside me—
Still grooving to that tune.

The old philosopher, dying,
Writes a last brief essay
In which he confesses
He wishes he'd learned
More poems by heart.

"The old chestnuts,"
He calls them,
By which he means
The rhyming ones
He loved when young.

"I would have been more
Fully human," he writes.

Reciting, in his last days,
Those he remembers,
As if the Book
Were in his mind,
And he was reading them aloud

Which is the resurrection
Of the body of the beloved,
Which is the world.

(in memoriam: Richard Rorty)

Doesn't the world demand
We dance?
Doesn't it insist on it?
And why not?
                    Look
At the leaves,
Look at the weeds.
Look at the least blade
Of grass in the breeze.

None of them begs off
Or offers excuses.

None of them refuses.

If you believe Shakespeare's
Sonnet, the beloved's
"An ever-fixed mark"—
A still star ships can steer by,
Something unwavering.

To me, the beloved's more
Like that Chinese fable
Where a man boarded
An empty raft floating by
And was swept downstream
To the sea and from there up
Into the River of Heaven.

And even aloft, in final
Star-form, he didn't stay
In a single spot but
Wandered.
                And still
Wanders, following his own heart.

Sun-drenched, late
August days
Ripening
The blackberries
Along the driveway.

Avoiding the briars,
Leaning over
The stalks and
Pushing aside
The yellowing leaves . . .

Each morning,
The tart juice
Turning a little
Sweeter
As the fruit darkens.

Which is the beloved,
Which is the world.

Time is a wound that can't
Close—it flows, it flows.

All that's begotten rots—
It's not anything
Personal the world
Has against us—
That's the way it goes.

Tune we first heard
In our mother's womb
And never even asked
If it was sad or happy,
Because we knew it was true.

River inside the river.
World within the world.

All we have is words

To reveal the rose
That the rose obscures.